THE FISH TH...

Elizabeth MacLennan

*for dear Jody, who keeps waving wonderfully, o not drowning..!
with love from
Elizabeth x*

LIVE CANON

First Published in 2013
By Live Canon Ltd
www.livecanon.com

978-1-909703-00-1

Edited by Helen Eastman for Live Canon
Visit www.livecanon.com to find out more about our books, CDs, podcasts and live
poetry events.

THE FISH THAT WINKED

Elizabeth MacLennan was born and grew up in Scotland, in Glasgow and in the Highlands. She studied music, then read Modern History at Oxford University and trained as an actor at LAMDA (The London Academy of Music and Dramatic Arts).

After ten years of successful freelance work in theatre, TV and films, mostly working with new writers, she was, with John McGrath, co-founder of the two 7:84 theatre companies, in England and Scotland. There followed twenty-five years of touring such shows as *The Cheviot, The Stag and The Black, Black Oil*, *Little Red Hen, Men Should Weep, The Baby and the Bathwater* and, later, five 'solo epic' shows for Freeway Stage and Floodtide, such as *Watching for Dolphins, Wild Raspberries* and *HyperLynx* (McGrath's last play, 2002). They travelled to theatres and halls all over Britain, Ireland, Europe and Canada, from the Outer Hebrides to Tblisi to Cape Breton.

She was married to John McGrath and they have three children. He died in 2002 of leukaemia. She continues to write, teach, travel and to cherish her growing tribe of grand-children. Based now in London, she spends time in Greece and the Highlands.

By the same author:

The Moon Belongs to Everyone (Making Theatre with 7:84): Methuen

Wild Raspberries – an epistolatory play: Fairplay Press

Ellie and Granny Mac – a story for children: Walker Books

Eliza et ses deux grand-mères (folio cadet): Gallimand Jennesse

This is her first collection of poems.

With love to my friends in Scotland, in Ithaca and elsewhere.

Thanks to my amazing extended family, immediate when needed and never a drag. Bob, the generous enabler – carpe diem! Kenneth, my shoulder-brother, listener, for his unflinching-support and approval. Likewise David, inspirer of another generation – keep writing songs!

Finn, the hero, peacemaker, befriender, film-maker, my first born...

Dan, bullshit-buster, prime dad, magic storyteller – make more movies!

Kate the Great, my girlchild, show spinner, heart stopper, wisdom imparter, beauteous baby-maker – blessings to you all.

To their help meets – Helen, Sue, Juliet, Franny, Sophie, Tom – YOU ARE THE ONES! – hurray! Love and big thanks.

To my darling grand-children – Hannah, Ella, Scarlett, Eliza, Jamie and Jack – who might even read them one day – all my love.

Thanks for their early confidence to Olga Taxidou and John Clement. Huge thanks to Jenny Prior, friend and encourager, for tackling my hand-writing, my insecurity, and processing them with gaiety and no complaint.

Especial thanks to Helen Eastman, friend-like-a-daughter, my enthusiastic editor, who said 'this will make an incredible collection' and did it.

And appreciative thanks to ALL at Live Canon for everything they have done.

THE FISH THAT WINKED

Contents

Two for the New Year

1. In the Highlands

When you build a peat fire,
you must never let it die,
but every night, lay gently
on some more, that's hard and dry,

so that in the morning, when you wake,
before you drink some tea,
there are glowing embers in the hearth
re-kindled – love from E ...

2. Sweethearts

Write it in pebbles on the sand,
in letters ten feet high,
in soap bubbles, on frosty panes,
in plane trails in the sky.

Scratch it on walls of churches,
near ancestors long gone,
in ashes where the fire has died:
Elizabeth loves John.

Leave-taking

I watched my love departing from his life
which was so precious to him.
'My life is very precious to me, I shall miss you all.'
He smiles, and turns away his head -
'We're fine.' 'D'you think I'll die of this tonight?'
'A bad idea, not suitable at all! I need some sleep –
Sing me a song, instead!' He does, John McCormack:

Just a song at twilight, when the lights are low,
And the evening shadows softly come and go.
Though the heart be weary, sad the night and long,
Still to us at twilight, comes love's old song...

'I think I need to leave you now, if it's all right?'
'Of course,' I say, 'I'm here for you to go.'
That smile -

His pale boat, tied up by the glassy shore,
the painter in my hand no longer strains
as through my fingers, imperceptibly, it slips
into the water, floating gently from the sandy shore
into the still blue sea, white sand below
a pale dragonfly,
and with loving, whispered breath, was gone.
So little time it took, but oh, forever
his gentle heart stopped beating.

Winter

My love is in his workroom,
he sits there every day,
he's reading or he's writing
but he won't come out to play.

My love is in the garden,
he's sitting in the chair,
nothing in particular
he's mostly doing there.

My love is in the wardrobe,
his pens are stiff with rust,
his shoes are in the Oxfam shop
gathering dust —

I saw him in the subway,
elegant and slim,
but when he turned towards me
I could see it wasn't him.

He isn't in the theatre,
they're doing other plays,
many haven't heard of him —
these are different days.

His century has been and gone,
his books are on the shelf,
no message on the ansaphone,
there's one I made myself.

He isn't in the bookshop
where he always was before,
he isn't in the cinema,
or walking on the shore.

I ask him what he thinks of things
and usually he's right,
he's not there in the morning
and he's never there at night.

My love is in the graveyard,
he's underneath the ground,
he's lying in the valley
where the peewits sound.

He doesn't hear the traffic,
he doesn't smell the rose,
they drink a lot of whisky
when a man like him goes.

Let's Get Wellied

Let's get wellied, bevvied, banjaxed,
Guttered, fleein', hammered, smashed. Let's
Give out, put the world tae rights 'n
Show the bastards. Let's get lashed.

Who di they think they ur, the government –
Think we'll no notice whit they're at?
We're getting poorer, harder, meaner
Naebody's bothered, rich 'n fat.

Saw this show wi ma mate at a theatre,
Christ, didnae want tae - they're aw mad,
John Maclean 'n stuff wis in it,
Made me laugh, it wis no half bad.

Blokey dressed as a bird wis singin',
Lassie wis the drummer in a red top hat.
We had a rerr time, right, no kiddin' –
When we were oot sumday smashed up ma flat.

On Tour In Belgium

Uts pushn doonin Antwerp[1]
fulla fermers boisn gurls[2]
trayun tae be smert[3]
"Flemfulm[4]", ledbak, 'n' a
naebdy tae speke tae[5]
whaursma jing?[6]
Wanna freen.[7]
Mammy![8]

---

[1] Scots dialect for 'It's rather wet in Antwerp'
[2] Scots dialect for 'Full of farmers boys and girls'
[3] Scots dialect for 'Trying to be clever'
[4] A reference to a Flemish film festival
[5] Scots dialect for 'Nobody to talk to'
[6] Scots dialect for 'Where's my girl?'
[7] Scots dialect for 'I want a friend'
[8] Scots dialect for 'Mummy!' The speaker is clearly distressed.

The Builders are In

I am clenched like a fist
to cope once more
with death, floods, no money,
no water, no heat, sandstorms of dust.

I try to find it funny.

Five men, or six, blast through my house,
they work, they turn it over,
they tell me things can only get better,
I pack up boxes, try not to hover.

I have a poem in my head...
it can't get out, my brain is dead,
turn off the radio, I plead –
too late, the poem's gone to seed –

I'll make a pot of tea for two,
it seems the only thing to do,
I'll crack a joke, they'll raise a smile,
I'll try to find that missing file.

Inventory

Need to fix the wardrobe,
Need to fix the door,
Need to fix the rotten window -
sill, the creaky floor.
Need to fix the dripping tap,
the outside light, the gate,
Need to read the rest of Proust
before it is too late -
no he can wait, he'll still be there
when I am gone beyond,
And then I'll come back organised
(as well as rich and blonde -)
no safety pins will fix my skirt,
my nails will shine, my mind
will be as vacant as a park
the circus left behind.
My beaux will be solicitous,
they'll open every door,
the world will be unruffled,
just like it was 'before' -
stones will stay unturned,
and the wind of change won't blow
our lives about in fragments
as we strive to have a go
at living, working, struggling,
small ways to leave some mark,
has anyone seen my glasses?
I am groping in the dark.

Festive Edinburgh

Summer comes grudgingly to Edinburgh.

Grey gloves still stick out of the woolly drawer,
socks from Harris, wait for the east wind to pounce.

While softies in Glasgow enjoy their sleeveless sun –
fresh faced cotton socked pin-cushion heids –
whaur's yer cloth cap the noo –
we, festive, glower up through fifty feet of haar.

Wifies scowl disapproval and wipe
non-existent dog shite off their already brown shoes.
Could that young person be enjoying herself?
We're not put here for that, good grief,
life's not a bus shelter,
what do they all expect?
This is a granite faced wind tunnel,
Dundas Street, nine a.m.

Public Funding for the Arts
(Notes Taken at a Theatre Conference)

Product, admin costing venue,
market grid promote expand,
hype, success, control, cost-effective,
insist guidelines, cut, redress
balance, better-placed financial
single unit image, maximize
flagship a – pol – i – t – i – cal.

Inspect quality, access, process
in committee, application,
turnover six-hundred million, rising,
centres of excellence
maintain fabric –
have you tried the British Council ... ?

Carpe Diem

My courteous Jordanian neighbours offered tea –
they are anxious to cut down our sycamore tree.
The sycamore gives courtyard shade, which pleases,
but keeps the sun off more delightful species –
like the lilac, soft and scented, and the cherry,
even holly might produce a scarlet berry.
Now it's done, the grass is greener still,
especially since they kindly paid the bill.

Mrs Don Juan

Mrs Don Juan lives in an ordinary flat,
she empties the cat litter, throws out the cat,
she cleans out the lavvy, mops up the floor,
reads Cosmopolitan, slumped by the door.

She wears fluffy slippers with broken down wedges,
hangs out her sheets, and dusts her edges,
the sunbed's her treat – the humming, the heat –
she closes her eyes to the noise from the street.

Mrs Don Juan started life Miss San Sebastian –
she likes to get back there whenever she can.
But little Don Juan keeps her on the go -
he has to have everything – well, just so.

But she dreams of a little cariña,
to dress in white frills and gardenias...

Heading South

Driven by rain
from rivet and privet
we come to stare
at the prickly pear.

Show Business

It's the luck of the draw
or who you know
where you'll end up, Euphemia –
on the end of the pier at Morecambe
or filming in Southern Bohemia.

Gypsies at Methoni
(Filming in Greece)

They came in the rain
bursting rainbows
gold-dusted cheeks, black-eyed babies slung behind,
children darting,
vermillion red shawls and bundles.

We faded, pale metropolitan people
beside their gaudy splendour.
The children ate everything and went
piled in a clapped out lorry,
to the Mani, or Tashkent.

Loneliness

If I sit very still with my back to the wall
and avoid the goat-shit
in the castle farmyard
I can learn a bit of Czech
and think about a poem
but if I get talking I won't do much.
If I ignore the chatter and the giggles
I can sit with a prune face
and stare out of the window
and wish I were somewhere else.

Sorrel

I had a story when I was a child
with a heroine called Sorrel.
I liked the name,
strong, unusual, not pretty pretty –
independent,
maybe when I became a successful writer
I'd be Sorrel Ross.

Here in Bohemia near the Austrian border
Sorrel is everywhere,
she blushes in every lush meadow and hedgerow,
she is best friends with cow parsley
and buttercup,
she glows and shines in the tall grass.
She looks down on clover
but clover is sweet, while Sorrel tastes bitter.

Vyssi Brod

Vyssi Brod is to Bohemia
what Dalkeith is to the Lothians -
the armpit.

But some people go to Dalkeith
for their holidays.

Anyway, the cups and saucers
come from China.

The Fall of Winnie Mandela

The South African police
use invisible ink for blackening.
When you wipe down the wall with tears –
bloodstains appear.

They will take everything they can from Winnie,
they will give her Nelson, then take him away, again,
they will take her shining reputation,
they will take her sleep, and her liberal friends.

When freedom comes, Winnie will laugh,
But she will cry at night, alone.

The Clown and the Dancer

The clown is waving, smiling
the clown is saying goodbye
soon all he has of the dancer
will be the look he remembers in her eye
a wisp of hair as she passes
a heart that stopped a beat
a hand that she took away from his
the sound of passing feet.

The clown is standing on the roadway
her carriage has long gone
he winks at a passing lizard
he feels no heat from the sun
the children will always love him
they laugh and cluster around
but this creature is gone beyond him
his feet are dull on the ground.

Normalice
(Normalization)

The Russians did it to the Czechs,
Czechs to Tziganes,
Americans to the Vietnamese
Iraqis to Kurds
Nazis to Jews
Generals to campesinos
Boer to black
Multinationals to poor farmer/docker/miner
Some women to some children
Some children to some other children
Some toddlers to some babies.
It's normal, innit.

Scarlett

The Kermes oak
which can be found
at Can Blanc
is the ancient source
of crimson. On its leaves
tiny insects yield the precious dye,
for Doge and cardinal to wear
beside their voluptuous wives and courtesans.
So, in the shelter of Can Blanc,
a new renaissance grew,
serenaded by cicada, owl and frogs,
near olive, vine and almond, fig and pear
came fair and precious, much-prized Scarlett
and all were joyful there.

Pied Wagtail

I am a wagtail
black and white,
delicate,
I move purposefully
in no particular direction –
small, busy, scurrying,
I don't hang about,
I get on with it.

Some people think I'm pretty
in an absent-minded sort of way.
I frequent mountainous districts
with meadows and wild flowers,
I am domestic,
I mind my own business.
My partner is never far away
sometimes alongside
usually separate.

Asini

Byzantine church, cinnamon smell
Beefeater gin bottle under the bell.

Tolo

Jasmine and fish smell on the shore
girl from South London, wanting more ...
cats jump out and scare
wish you were here.

Journeys

I came to Ithaki from the highlands,
the home of my people,
and its mist and rain.
We have sunsets too, even sunshine
which is not expected by the tourists
who come looking for Rob Roy and Braveheart
and the mythical monster in Loch Ness.

Travelling with a theatre troupe for two decades,
we always journeyed on.
After each show, we danced and sang and left
never to fully arrive, or settle down.

So, in the terms set out by Cavafy
I am well qualified to journey to Ithaki
to go away and keep returning.
Now I am miso Exoyissana, half highland,
I take nothing for granted:
each day is a small miracle,
each full moon takes my breath away,
each departure a longed-for return,
each love is both an end and a beginning.

Three Bays

Polis

Polis is safe, a gentle-handed sea,
caressing, sleepy in the afternoon.
Loving too for families and exiles
delighted to catalogue the quality of the water
on this always special day,
before they leave reluctantly
for lunch, or sleep, or Australia.

Kourvouleia

The name is sexy, pouting, difficult to control.
She is rocky underfoot – BEWARE –
you might fall into her seductive arms
and be unable to leave them.
Stay, just a bit longer,
you will not regret it,
and she will still be there, luminous,
waiting for you to come again.

Afales

Afales is a stong-limbed woman,
she may put up a struggle,
darken, grow mysterious.
Wait for her on a calm day,
then take everything she offers,
it is not given lightly, she is
deep, deep, at times stormy, wild,
but when the moon is full
she is all you have ever hoped for.
Treat her with firmness and respect
and come to her as often as you can.
She is wide, wild, and waiting.

Why Odysseus Came Back

You can tell so much about a person
from how they eat a fig –
delicately, with curving tongue,
or plunging in, wide-mouthed, greedy
for every golden seed –
or in one quick, throaty gulp,
or languidly, section by section,
not leaving any out,
then neatly folding the flattened skin
not knowing quite where to put it...
Some eat the flesh, then chuck away the rest,
others gobble the lot, saving the skin
for one last delicious bite.

In England, in posh restaurants,
they serve them with a silver knife and fork,
maybe accompanied by cheese,
as if the thing itself were not enough.
Flown in from Greece or Turkey
the poor things are usually freezing cold,
not warm and succulent, melting,
bursting for it,
and dying to be invaded by man or wasp.

Ithaki is the place to eat figs properly –
either in July or early September,
cupping them gently in your hand,
ready to withdraw quickly from a wasp.

Apart from the odd dud,
it is a fig-eater's paradise.
Which is, of course, why Odysseus came back
in case Penelope had scoffed the lot
while he was making do with inferior dried up apricots
on offer from Calypso.

After the Tsunami
(the seismologist speaks candidly)

Morphology did indicate
transcontinental rupture,
a hundred times the energy –
we registered subduction –
the amplifying waves would reach
six hundred miles per hour,
uplifted area collapse
with displaced water power.
Although we all predicted
nothing else was put in place,
political inaction,
it's a worldwide disgrace,
we did not have the systems,
communications, men,
and now the odds are pretty high
it could occur again.
I cannot sleep at night, I feel
I should have done much more,
nothing quite so terrible has come my way before
- Christ, look at this, I said to Bill -
the seismogram was clear,
between ourselves, I doubt if I'll
be working here next year.

The Rough and the Smooth

Hammock of hills
hummock of thyme
hillock of rosemary –
mine, but not mine.

Vines trailing languorous
plums in cascade
gleaming gardenias –
rats on the raid.

Stamp on the cockroaches
creeping Darth Vaders
wherever there's Paradise –
bound to be raiders.

Autumn Crocus

In the musky woods
cyclamen like pink vulvae
promise everything.
Hidden among the dark leaves,
you have to look for them.
But I am a flashy autumn crocus,
bright yellow, I flaunt my charms
in the platia, people turn to stare,
old men in the cafeneion
wish they had been there.

Stormy Weather

Before the storm, my village in Ithaki
is like Arisaig in the Gaeltacht,
all silver streaks and gleaming,
thin veined clouds
receding distant islands, breathless
birds silenced,
pulsing earth, and hands arthritic,

then –
rumbling, rolling, crashing,
dripping roof, rain splashed in buckets
while overhead
the giant Polyphemus
turns his baleful eye towards Lefkada,
to stride across the hilltop and the sea
in their direction.

Indoors, snug, my fire hisses,
fir-cones winking,
I am shuttered tight.

Book parcel to collect from Thea Titika
when the rain stops.

Lone Cicada

The sun was definitely out today
shining on the scene.
The sky was blue, the water calm
the atmosphere serene

and then he started –
the lone cicada
defiant questioning
energetic, noisy
irrepressible, hot-blooded –
that did it.

He sang so lustily all day,
I knew that not so far away
his brothers and sisters were singing in the sun,
every one joyfully cacophonous
without a thought for all of us.

Sing on sing on, til summer's gone
and drown, rottweilers, drown,
yours is the smile on summer's face
that wipes out winter frown.

On hearing the words 'I love you'

Now I am a leaping hare,
the fish that winked on the marble slab,
the foetal heartbeat,
the hole in the smooth pebble in your pocket,
a moving comet in the night sky,
the candle flame that stayed alight
on the windy walk home.

I am all jasmine.
I gleam in the dark.
I am the breath of morning,
I am the sudden memory of things to come.

Winter Evening in the City

Looking for metaphors on a London bus
I think only of the smell of melons, ice, and us.

Promises, promises ...

Tomorrow afternoon
I'll be
a ripe plum –
(if you come ...)

A prune
will be
your fate
if you are late.

Giving

Give all

      expect nothing

            no blame

Hope forever

      laughter tears

            no shame

Sweet loving

      separation

            play the game

Satisfaction in the moment

      you were there

            when he came.

Observed at a Distance

I watch you eating small fish
with great deliberation.
You lift them tenderly
to your lovely mouth
while emphasizing a point
to your guest – with the other finger –
you pop them deliciously and sexily
into your plum purple mouth.

I notice you are much thinner,
your lovely elbows which I liked to kiss
are thin, your hands seem fragile,
hair longer, eyes veiled, hooded.
Having ensured that I will not embarrass you,
you are pointedly not looking in my direction.
You are wearing the faded red t-shirt
I might steal from you, one day soon.

The people you are lunching with are tired of life,
but you are not, not yet.
The parents are impressed by you, and by this place.
You are mildly bored, but always polite,
the girl is tense, could well be frigid –
They are careful. About money. About life.
He has lost his hair. What's left is scraped over the top
of his dull skull and regulated brain.

I must admit I'm not a bit excited.

A Wish

I wish you to think about me
when you are all alone,
or when you're with lots of people
or when they are all gone.

I wish it makes you smile
to know I think of you,
I wish to make you laugh out loud
- even to make you frown.

Lunch Time

Together, alone,
is almost as good as together together.
There is anticipation, excitement,
wonder. There is an air of peace.
It is a kind of truce.
Getting ready, without getting ready.
I am a clear sea,
you can see all the way to the stones
on the bottom.
I am a cat, waiting for the fishbones.
With luck, I might get something more.
But it is a mistake
to believe in promises, cat.

Hoping

I don't give up hope
even on windy nights
with bad dreams of stabbings
and babies being injured
falling off beds
I don't ...
Give up

I believe in hope
in energy
in optimism of the will
in the wind in my face
blowing away misery

There is a fair amount
to be sorry about ...
Mostly the waste, the time passing
opportunities offered
and not seized -

That person I observe
sees things differently...
For the moment he's pre-occupied
so none of this is relevant
not the time or the place
or the optimism
(perhaps some dreaming)
but for now
I am not the problem
nor the solution.

Happier Mood

Looking for pebbles with a hole in them,
- of course I wanted two, one for each of us.

In the afternoon (when I had stopped looking)
I found them, well-matched, side by side.
Delighted, I gave you yours the next day
to keep – maybe to hide.

So one day, when you are least expecting,
it might turn up, your pebble,
in a jacket you haven't worn
for a while.

You might smile.
And a friend of yours might say –
You look happier today –

The Wall and the Lizard

Quite soon after the earthquake, cracks
began to appear in the wall. Relax,
the lizard thought, it is strong enough.
But then pieces broke away, and stones crumbled.
She was quite badly hurt,
and there was no sun to heal her scars,
so she fled, looking for a place of safety.

Out of Joint

I lie on a massage bed,
my head is being manipulated
by the hands of a sensitive young Australian woman –
her Greek father came from a village somewhere near Larissa,
she tells me, but she grew up in Melbourne.
"Ah," I say, "the second city of Greece."
"Why did so many of them leave?" she asks
'Well," I say, "there wasn't quite enough to go around,
and the Brits let them down, after the war,
and there was civil war, reprisals, fascism,"
"What is fascism?" she asks me blankly, "I know nothing about –
you seem to know about - political things - "
"Dictatorship," I say, "no elections? prison camps?
ironical in the birth place of democracy?"
She is silent, feeling for displaced vertebrae.
        I am waiting for things to click,
        for things to fall into place.

Missing Persons

1. Easter Thursday

Inside my local church it is quite ugly
but it is quiet
set back from the busy High Street.

I will go to the big cathedral perhaps, tonight,
and think about the Last Supper.
I will pray for those I loved and lost
and those I love and have not lost,
I will pray for you in the lost and found section.
I will light a candle
I will be very tired.

On the way home, I will look at the moon.
It is hard to believe in miracles
but I am a believer,
I trust and am trusted,
I am innocent, a bit out of this world.

2. My Secret

My secret is in the lily,
which smells of partings,
it is the first star of the evening,
the rain on the dirty pavement,
exhaustion on the face of the Chinese woman
on the bus, the legs of the old man
clutching his plastic bag.
My mouth is ready for you, bruised,
I am an open book, turned face down,
abandoned by the reader,
I am tucked beneath your pillow,
you are leaning on my hair
your elbow is in my back
your face is icon-stern, grave,
I look for it at the station,
in the dark, waiting for the show to begin,
no tears now, only aching –
my secret sadness. My lost love.

Looking at Gwen John's room in Paris, 1907

It is an attic room.
She has only just come in from the street.
It is a late summer evening.
There are flowers on the table, but they are not in the middle.
In the middle of the picture is the sloping ceiling,
it leans towards her bed, which we cannot see.
Everything is muted.
The window is veiled, and its view shadowy.
There is a feeling of emptiness, but also, faint anticipation.
On the brown cushion, there is light from the evening sun,
it might be a warm place to sit.
The room is waiting for someone to appear.
She will move her umbrella to the corner,
she will sit down and put on her shawl,
she will listen to the noises from the street,
she will get up and straighten the sheets,
then she will sit down again and wait,
      hands folded.

Snow

Snow falling

cold nights

logs splutter

street lights

Silence falling

inside my head

thoughts blown against the wall

like leaves, dead.

The Ornithologist Explains

Among the smaller birds,
Spring comes earliest for the robin.
Even in December,
while others huddle round the fire,
he is already looking for his mate.

His partner-to-be is off, travelling far,
she is carefree in her independent status,
but generally, she will return to an exact spot
she has already marked out in October.

Has she marked him out as well?
We do not know this. It's possible,
but we know, from tagging, that she has her eye
on the nesting place, and frequently returns.

On seeing her, his song becomes excited,
beautifully ornate.
After a little, if you listen now, you will hear her reply.
She has noticed him.
Now he is murmuring, quietly pleased.
Then afraid perhaps she will not stay
he becomes urgent with arpeggios
singing his heart out. It is very seductive.
And all this before the end of January.

Foreboding

Now that the waiting's nearly over
I am sad.
Perhaps the reality will be bleak
and not glad.
Perhaps a distance, even,
certainly a sense of loss,
my passion put in its place
and everything will pass

Horizon

Looking anxiously astern
you cannot see
shimmering prospects ahead.
Cast off from that hospitable shore
where once or twice you sheltered happily.

The wind has changed
another vessel has berthed there,
your moorings were easily transferred,
fishes dart beneath another hull
it's much the same to them.

The old trawler has company alongside,
the sun is up, make the most of it
slip out to sea, quietly,
with a soft following wind.

Exit Strategy

It is with extreme regret
that we write to inform you
that our client wishes to sever
her relationship.
She finds that, on balance
the odds are heavily weighed
against her interest.
In spite of repeated attempts
to rectify this situation
she has met with an almost entirely
negative response.
This, admittedly, has been confused
by sporadic fits of short-lived enthusiasm,
even protestations of extreme desire
to have further contact,
but these outbursts have amounted
to nothing, or at best, distress.
Having made several attempts
to meet and discuss these matters
for the benefits of both parties,
and having been repeatedly rebuffed,
she will not consider any further offers
from the party in question, at this time.

Anti-Inflammatory

Lugging suitcase of books to
small ferry boat, down bumpy jetty,
winding in taxi, down through rough overgrown hillside,
to damp-jammed door, push, lift,
shove, clean, paint, climb step-ladder,
sweep floor, bend, twist, carry buckets –
of course my back hurts.
Bring on the anti-inflammatories.

Now in a gentle haze of paracetemol
(and local wine ...)
I contemplate the green sweet mother sea below.

Beyond the sea, banks burn in Athens, people die.
Elections at home, too early to say –
I wait for the parties to get into bed together.

In Iceland that volcano still erupts.
Europe is blanketed in ash
and only birds can fly.
Beware: Icarus was overconfident, cocky –
the first sub-prime fantasist to crash.

The Goat with One Horn

He is lofty, surveys the rest,
knowing he's unique.
Was it an accident
or a defective gene?
Whatever, who cares, he has the pick
of all the boys and girls,
one butt in the butt
and they're madly frisky.

He munches sage with sagacity,
he has the capacity.
It's cool now. The night is young,
the herd shimmy on falling rocks.
He looks the other way,
time enough ...

Leaving Ithaki

You cannot take it with you,
the images fade, the sounds of goat-bells
disappear in London's traffic.
The exact blue-green of the sea today
at September's end, after the storm,
cannot be fully recalled, even in an hour or two,
the silk caressing sea between your legs
washes away in the first bathtub,
police sirens will drown out the sounds of owls,
starry nights dimmed by city flares.
So.
Pack up every scribbled note, cds,
letters, honey carefully wrapped, small white stones,
five lemons, still green,
basil, rigani and lavender –
when I open the case, island smells come back
to haunt me for a week or two –
till Christmas they might linger in that pocket.
Calamity is looming in Greece,
my friends are fraught and anxious
knowing there is little they can do.
I can feel the danger but
my water tank is full,
I have some food, wine, and, tomorrow
if it stays sunny, one last swim.

Flashback

'My friend the seagull came to see me,'
says Danny, on the white bed
in the Cherry Orchard hospital, Dublin,
where his tree nearly fell. Aged six.
We watch the black rooks circling outside his window,
the slow-changing clouds. 'I like that sky.'
We have our evening ritual, hold hands, kiss goodnight,
another story...
God is good, says Bernie, tucking up.
I fill the white jug with fresh water,
now in the fourth good day.
We listen to the great Caruso, at Mary Murphy's fireside,
with wizard cloaks and hats for Hallowe'en.
On a trip to the fair, Finn gets picked up by an elephant!
'Who were the best Irish writers, mama?' says he, the hero...
'Sean O'Casey, Beckett, Brendan Behan?' says I,
mighty relieved. God...

Back in Edinburgh now, the streets still smell of coal.
It rains for days.
We put white bulbs in the black soil, wellies mucky.
'Not a good day for gardening, tut,' our neighbour,
lips pursed, clucky. I shrug a nod,
the boys intent upon the coming spring,
the sun on our backs, some heat,
lighter the long evenings, playing football in the street.

A Good Match

She's the bee in his honey
the laces in his boots
he's the text in her message
they've inter-twining roots

He's the salt in her pepper
she's the fizz in his champagne
in their loving republic
neither shall reign

Pomegranates

To be a well-versed pomegranate-eater
you should dream in colours,
red, coral and gold.
It is the fruit for you, my dear,
take your pick with care,
then clasp the goblet tenderly
not spilling any drops of juice.

Now comes the heady swift embrace, plunge
face to face, urgent
mouth to sweetest mouth
tongue, lips, seeds, pith.

Later, smiling, milky-eyed,
take your time with the entrée,
prepared and chosen carefully
it will not disappoint,
enough to satisfy your lusty appetite
yet leave you wanting more...

The Waiting Game

No way of knowing what's in store,
maybe a gentle fade to black
with no subtitles . . .

Or passing in the street:
how are you? Well? And quickly
on his way, resolute, swift.

Or: you won't believe how busy,
too much, too much,
I'm afraid impossible for several weeks,
I'll be in touch, I wish you all the very best.

Or, suddenly: hello, how are you?
May I see you perhaps on Friday?
What time, is early good for you?
I know you need your beauty sleep,
I look forward . . .

Or in the café, surrounded by
discussion, enclosed world,
no flicker of recognition (though I know
he spotted me crossing the street).
Later: you looked ravishing . . . maybe next Friday?

A Cup of Coffee

Here there is plenty to do
but nothing to be done.
The sun is shining, sea is blue
the green hillside tumbling flowers
the view clear to far distant other islands.

In the city, volcanic ash above, general strike below.
No ferries will sail today
no planes will plough the skies,
birds sing, the sea is calm, whispering,
my house is damp after a long wet winter,
throw wide the doors and shutters,
hang everything out to dry,
sit on my eyrie-balcony and watch small birds,
small sails on the sea below.
A pile of books is waiting, yet to read,
there is water, cheese, olives, two lemons on my trees,
a fish, some wine, goat bells, tomatoes –
and coffee, from my friend.
Open the carefully sealed packet from my suitcase -
ah, the aroma is sharp with memory,
coffees drunk to savour our pleasure together
(his gravitas in the preparation...)

More unpacking reveals a book given for my birthday
the inscription catches my breath, 'carpe diem'.
Yes of course of course!
and tight wrapped in my sweater, a delicate photo frame –
Later, after a glass or two of garnet-red wine,
I might kiss the space which holds no photograph,
wishing you a happy month of best behaviour,
and good fortune to come again,
persona grata, dear persona grata
never innammorata.

Fat Chance

I like to think of all the smooth romantic ladies
Whose smug melodious passage through lyric poetry and prose
Would be jarred forever by such an unlovely,
Unsung complaint as mine at present,
Ah, Mumps!
The Lady of Shalott, for instance,
La Belle Dame sans Merci clearly sans mumps as well –
Or shingles – there's another unsung malady...
No knights bedazzled would ride forth and bring back potions -
Sir Fingal for the Lady of the Scarlet Shingles, a battle trophy -
Scabs, bunions, athlete's foot of course
Would have really fucked things up for Persephone.

Having mumps, like falling on a banana skin,
Is strictly for the Beano.
It's easier to imagine it on
Mother Courage, or Gracie Fields,
Or maybe even Sylvia Pankhurst -
Gorki's mother probably had it every other week
And never turned a hair,
Joan Littlewood could obviously cope with it
And Gold Meir -
And if I may be serious for a moment
Rosa Luxemburg survived much worse, for a time...
Than mine... so all in all,
With a regretful backward glance
At my delicious girlhood heroines –
Languid, lovely, and always in control –
I guess I'll throw my lumpen lot in,
With the pirotted and begrotten.

Some hae luck, and some hae trumps
And some puke in a bucket.
But I hae collyshangin' mumps
And sae I'm fairly fuckit.

Keep the Shows Coming
(for Kate)

It's grey today –
a lighter grey than yesterday,
but no sign of the mean reds
let alone the blue blues,
just leaking shoes, another war
and winter piety,
no variety.

So – lets make woopee
doop-di-doopy,
let's tell stories, daft and gory,
let's set the world to rights
let's sit up and talk all nights
we have the skills, the words, the lights
we have the talent
and the nerve
let's give them
what they deserve.

Poetry School

In the brochure, everyone is smiling
the women poets cheerfully drink coffee,
bonding in groups, so no panic –
like an ante-natal class.
The men fly solo, straight to camera
like proper writers.

It says there are beginners' classes, Master class
(names to be confirmed),
tutorials, seminars, it says
be prepared, bring something to read:

THERE WILL BE VERSIFICATION
BE PREPARED TO WRITE SOMETHING DURING THE
WORKSHOP.

Did they ask Homer how would you describe
your ethnic origin?
Some days he just looked at the waves,
at the perfect oval white stone
with a small rounder one beside it,
before drinking coffee (not tidying up his desk)
and then embarked, reluctantly, on another voyage
- or stayed in bed, his hands behind his head,
watching the sun paint ladders on the ceiling.

Re-cycling for the New Year

This old cigar box with its Moorish border
at first embraced some heady Montecristos (No.4).
I liked inhaling the aroma, while others smoked
and planned to change the world.
For many years it's lain neglected in that dusty cupboard
with some unpronounceable liqueur from Prague.

Now, redding up for the approaching Year,
I fish it out. One last cigar remains
dry, musky smell, disintegrating in my hand.
Folding Christmas ribbons, so much gentler to the touch,
I linger dully on their brilliant reds,
their languorous abandonment.
This is the place for them, the flame,
the tartan, baby pink, and gold,
the wine-coloured with silver edges
now nestle there, rolled slowly on my forefinger.
They will not come undone, hunched close together.
By next New Year, some others
may have turned up, lying around
like flashes of sunlight on a January day.

Tahrir Square

I am waiting for another friend to die,
I am anticipating this good red wine on the back of my throat,
I am waiting for a vast electricity bill to arrive,
I am anticipating your smiling arrival,
I am waiting for this power drill to stop,
I am anticipating your hearty laughter,
I am waiting for this crisis to be over,
I am waiting to be betrayed,
I am anticipating ecstasy,
I am waiting in the rain for two tardy buses,
I am anticipating the smell of peat and jasmine,
I am waiting for the next avoidable cliché to pass me by,
I am anticipating the aroma of gardenias,
I am waiting to be 'put on hold', and for the death of musak,
I am anticipating a plate of gleaming sardines,
I am waiting for my leg to heal, and for my heart to heal,
I am anticipating achieving the impossible,
I am eagerly anticipating the next revolution ...

Keep Well

Lying alone, without a nurse,
in a hopefully sterile hospital,
lying alone in a police station cell – is all very well.

Both warmed by a dim blue light.
Everything could possibly be all right?

You could bang on the door,
but I wouldn't advise it.
Nobody in their right mind tries it.

Cold Comforts

Let's sit down –
here in my David Hockney painting
(no it wasn't in his recent exhibition).
His greens are unmistakeable though,
gleaming, don't you think?

So lucky, yes, I stumbled on it in a moment of despair,
well, not despair, not quite catastrophe
but well, depression, yes, and graphite skies,
in Greece of all places! Hardly what you would expect –
rummaging in the mind's eye -

His Yorkshire now, in May, would seem a paradise,
my Greek island glowering, few small birds, subdued,
short of water even despite the rain –

So underneath his burnished chestnut trees
beside the welcoming road that winds on to the highlands
let's settle to enjoy my bread and cheese and wine
bathed in his Yorkshire sunlight, languid shadows,
purple branches sprouting, my dreams beside me
laid out carefully on his tree stump –
a sleepy afternoon, we'll doze among the bees
and later as the shadows grow and dusk begins to fall
we'll set off for the far north and the tall sunset
the hills and lochs ahead, a quiet peaceful night, few cars.

Tomorrow sure the rain will move on to Arcadia
And fall on unsuspecting hikers fled from Hull.

The Imperfect Heart

To swim the Hellespont
requires a withered foot, like Byron,
whose other attributes outshone the god-like
if he and all his fans can be believed ...
Below that noble face, with its proud chin,
the slightest fold is touching, desirable
far beyond the perfect chiselled jaw of callow youth.
Those lines of pain, scepticism and laughter
bring warmth, forgiveness and humanity,
passion re-awakes.
To complete the other, imperfection is a prerequisite.
The cracked blue jug
blazes with marigolds.

Diagnosis

This part of my life
has already been written.
But I do not have a copy of the script.

It is, I suppose, a work in progress,
yet to be devised.

Various people are likely to contribute,
in unexpected ways.

There is a director
but he does not usually attend rehearsals.
They say he keeps an eye on things –
he has many other shows
he promises to be there for the curtain.
Typical. Trust him to stroll on,
smiling in his dinner suit
- on his way to some important supper
with important angels
- and take all the credit.

The audience won't be fooled.
If it goes well, they'll throw flowers
for me, grab a few drinks
and talk about it animatedly
on the way home.

Publication

If at first you don't succeed
make soup. Then at least you
don't have to eat your words.

For My Children

Gardenias,
Mozart,
mazurkas,
warm sea,
the smell of new books,
violets or 'love-in-idleness'
and always jasmine...

D-Day Commemoration on TV

How glorious we were,
how bravely our young men died
for their country. Now old men can
no longer bear the pain,
the pain of remembering,
of not being able to go for a piss,
while they line up in the freezing cold
for the Queen with her lavender hat
who walks slowly, slowly, with her wreath
so near but oh so far from the blood
spurting from your best mate's frightened eyes
that day in June, sixty years ago
when we were young and eager and shit-scared
and girl-nurses dragged bodies up the beach
fighting against fascism and knowing why.
The oil interests had not yet carved up the world
and there was – from time to time –
such a thing as freedom.

Surf Rider

See that amazing figure
on the silver board, breasting the wave gloriously,
then drowned in surf...
oh no, not quite, she reappears
miraculously...

How much more dangerous to live like this...
one minute, blackness, hopes dashed, then,
next, white wave adrenalin rush
you're off again, who knows –
or cares – where it will end –
until the next wall of terrifying water
brings ecstasy or oblivion.

Snapshot

Across a grassy English garden
decades ago – someone smoked a small cigar
clouds drifted – Sunday afternoon –
we could have been in Adlestrop,
daisies between my toes,
first baby sleeping on a blanket.

Now the smell of Fist mosquito coils
confirms beyond a doubt I'm back in Greece ...
warm skin, brown feet on the balcony rail,
almost a full moon, tinfoil stars,
a single bell below rings half past something ...

Soon, a new firstborn, this time for my daughter,
will lie sleeping on that rug,
wrapped in a shawl from Shetland.
My heart flutters and in the bay
a fish jumps. 'Mum, the baby's kicking.'
I'm on my way.

LIVE CANON